FLORIDA

in words and pictures

BY DENNIS B. FRADIN

ILLUSTRATIONS BY RICHARD WAHL

MAPS BY LEN W. MEENTS

Consultant
Wyatt Blassingame

CHILDRENS PRESS ™

CHICAGO

For My Father,
Myron Fradin, With Love

Mangrove Swamp, Mariana

For Their Help, the Author Thanks:
Dan Schafer, Associate Professor of History,
University of North Florida
at Jacksonville

Curtis Osceola, Director of Tribal Planning
Office, Miccosukee tribe of
Indians of Florida

Joe A. Quetone, Executive Director, Florida
Governor's Council on Indian Affairs

John Phelps, Executive Assistant to
the Speaker, Florida House of
Representatives

Edward Asper, Corporate Curator, Sea World

Library of Congress Cataloging in Publication Data

Fradin, Dennis B
  Florida in words and pictures.

  SUMMARY: Presents a brief history and descrip-
tion of the Sunshine State.
    1. Florida—Juvenile literature.
[1. Florida]   I. Wahl, Richard, 1939-
II. Meents, Len W.   III. Title.
F311.3.F72   975.9   80-16681
ISBN 0-516-03909-1

8 9 10 11 12 R 87 86

Picture Acknowledgments:
STATE OF FLORIDA, DEPARTMENT OF COMMERCE, DIVISION OF
TOURISM—pages 2, 5, 14, 16 (bottom), 17, 21, 22, 29, 30, 34, 35, 39, 41
JAMES P. ROWAN—8, 9, 18, 23, 24, 25, 27 (left), 28, 36, 37 (left), 38
JUDITH BLOOM FRADIN—19, 27 (right)
SEA WORLD—26
DADE COUNTY DEPARTMENT OF TOURISM—cover, 31, 32, 37 (right)
COURTESY OF MICCOSUKEE INDIAN RESERVATION—33
COVER PHOTO: The Atlantic Coast

Florida

If you were in a spaceship high above Earth, it would be easy to spot Florida. It hangs like a stocking in the far southeastern United States.

Florida has warm weather the year round. It has so much sunshine that it is nicknamed the *Sunshine State.* Warmth and sunshine make Florida a fine place for growing fruit. The orange juice you drink in the morning may come from Florida. Florida is the leading state for growing oranges.

People, too, like Florida's warm weather! Millions vacation there in the winter. Baseball teams train in the state. Many older people have gone there to live.

Do you know where the oldest town in the United States is located? Or where the first spaceship to the moon was launched? Do you know what state's name means *full of flowers?* Or where you can see alligators in a place called the Everglades?

If you haven't guessed, the answer to all these questions is: Florida!

Long before people lived in Florida, there were interesting animals. Saber-toothed tigers prowled about. Their teeth were six inches long. Mastodons were there. They looked like big, hairy elephants. There were small kinds of horses and camels. None of these are alive today. But their bones have been found in many places.

The first people came to Florida at least 10,000 years ago. Early people made spears and hunted in Florida's forests. They fished in the ocean. Their stone tools and weapons have been found.

The oldest house in St. Augustine

Indians may be related to these early people. The
Indians farmed. They grew corn, squash, and beans.
They hunted with bows and arrows. They also fished.
The Apalachee (ap • ah • LAY • chee), Timucua (tim • ah •
KOO • ah), Calusa (kah • LOO • sah), and Tequesta (teh •
QUES • tah) were four of the main tribes in Florida.

The Spanish came in the early 1500s. They were the first known explorers to arrive. One, Ponce de León, lived in Puerto Rico. He heard stories about a land to the northwest. This land was supposed to have gold. It was also said to have magical water. "By taking a drink of the water, an old man can become young again!" people said. The water was called the *Fountain of Youth.*

Ponce de León sailed from Puerto Rico. In 1513 he arrived in a land he called *Florida* (meaning *full of flowers* in Spanish). He didn't find the Fountain of Youth or gold. However, he did explore the land. He claimed Florida for Spain.

Ponce de León left Florida, but came back in 1521. This time he tried to form a colony. He and his men started to build houses. The Indians knew that these outsiders wanted their land. The Indians attacked. There

was a fierce battle. Ponce de León was wounded by a
poison arrow. He was taken to Cuba, where he soon died.

The Spanish badly wanted to control Florida. At this
time, Spanish ships sailed past Florida loaded with gold
and silver. If the Spanish ruled Florida, they could guard
the treasure ships from there. They tried a second time
to start a Florida colony. In 1559 about 1,500 people
were sent there by boat from Mexico. But they ran out
of food. The people had to eat their horses just to
survive. They were glad to leave.

Fort Caroline National Memorial

There was trouble for the Spanish in 1564. The French built a fort in northeast Florida. It was called Fort Caroline. The Spanish were afraid that the French would take control of Florida. In September of 1565 the Spanish tried once more to settle Florida. Pedro Menendez de Aviles (PAY • dro meh • NEN • dez DAY ah • VEE • lace) formed a settlement at St. Augustine. This time it lasted. St. Augustine was the first town formed in what is now the United States. Soon after founding St. Augustine, the Spanish drove the French out of Florida.

The old city gates
of St. Augustine

From St. Augustine, Spanish sailors guarded ships as they sailed by. But pirates sometimes robbed the ships. St. Augustine was also attacked by pirates a number of times. In 1586 the English sailor Sir Francis Drake burned St. Augustine. The city was rebuilt.

The Spanish built forts in Florida. There soldiers kept tight control of the land. Churches, called *missions*, were also built in Florida. There, priests taught the Indians about Christianity. They also taught them to grow crops and herd cattle. Few Spanish people wanted to settle in Florida, however. Most liked Mexico better.

Spain ruled Florida for almost 200 years. Then England and Spain fought a war. The war was not fought in Florida. But as part of the peace treaty in 1763, England took control of Florida. England ruled Florida from 1763 to 1783. Then, by another treaty, Spain took control again in 1783.

While Florida was bouncing around like a ping-pong ball, a new country was formed in America! This was the United States. People from the United States moved to Florida in the late 1700s and early 1800s. Most farmed. Cotton and sugar were main crops. As more Americans arrived, they wanted Florida to become part of the United States.

Spain was ready to give up Florida to the United States. But the Indians were not. There were two wars with the Indians before Florida became a state. They were called the First and Second Seminole Wars.

The Seminole Indians had lived in Georgia and
Alabama. But they were forced down into Florida in the
1700s. Many became farmers there. American settlers
wanted to force the Seminoles out of Florida and take
their lands. The Seminoles were beaten in 1818 in the
First Seminole War. But these proud people still
wouldn't leave their Florida homes.

Osceola, painted
by George Catlin

In 1835 the United States began fighting the Second Seminole War. Hundreds and hundreds of soldiers were sent in against the Indians. The Seminoles were led by a brave man named Osceola. After a fight, Osceola would hide his people in the swamps of southern Florida. The Americans saw that they couldn't beat the Indians. Finally, the Americans tricked Osceola. They put up a flag of truce. They said that they wanted to talk to him. Instead, they captured Osceola and put him in prison. He died there. Although they were beaten badly, the Seminoles fought on until they were almost wiped out.

Seminole Indians live along the Tamiami Trail in the Florida Everglades.

They wouldn't stop fighting until they were given lands in southern Florida. Many still live there.

With Indian Wars ending, more and more people settled in Florida. By 1845 Florida had enough people to become a state. It became the 27th state on March 3rd of that year. Tallahassee was the capital.

Florida was called a "Slave State." That means slavery was allowed there. Some people had big farms, called *plantations*. Slaves did the work. Cotton and sugar were grown on the plantations.

Kingsley Plantation State Park

In the 1850s, Americans argued about slavery. People in Florida and the other Southern states feared that the U.S. government would end slavery. Southerners spoke of "States' Rights." They said each state should decide for itself about slavery and other issues.

War between the Northern and Southern states began. This was the Civil War (1861-1865).

Florida joined the Southern, or *Confederate,* (kon • FED • er • it) states. In 1864 Northern and Southern soldiers fought at a pond near Olustee (oh • LOU • stee). The

Southerners won the Battle of Olustee. In 1865 Northern
soldiers tried to capture the Florida capital of
Tallahassee. Northern soldiers landed in boats. They
headed for the capital. Southern soldiers met them at a
large rock called Natural Bridge. The Southern
soldiers—some of them Florida schoolboys and old men—
drove back the Northerners at the Battle of Natural
Bridge. Tallahassee was safe.

In other states the North won big battles. The North
had better supplies. It had more soldiers. In 1865 the
North won the Civil War. The slaves were freed.

In the late 1800s, cotton farming became less important in Florida. Some people tried growing oranges and grapefruits. These fruits need warm weather and good rainfall. Florida was perfect. More and more farmers turned to growing fruits. Fruit growing was on the way to becoming a giant business.

Above: Picking and loading oranges
Right: Citrus fruits ready to be sold

16

A pine tree

People also saw that Florida had huge forests of pines and other trees. Turpentine was taken from pine trees. Logging became important. Trees were cut. They were used to make wood products and paper. Logging is still done in the state today.

In the early 1900s, Florida sunshine brought thousands to the state. Retired people came to Florida to live. More and more farmers went there to grow oranges. In the winter, thousands went to Florida to vacation. Some liked the state so much they decided to stay!

Like oranges on a tree, new towns grew and grew. Miami, Fort Lauderdale, and Tampa were three of the growing towns.

Myakka River State Park

Florida has fine weather most of the time. But when the weather is bad it can be awful. Huge storms known as *hurricanes* form over the ocean. They hit land with winds over 75 miles per hour. They smash houses as if they were toys. They blow trains off their tracks. In 1928 a huge hurricane struck Florida, killing about 1,800 people. Big hurricanes struck Florida in 1935 and in other years.

Space vehicle display at the Kennedy Space Center

People can't stop hurricanes from coming. But they have learned how to protect themselves. Houses are built stronger now. Weather satellites in space take pictures of hurricanes. People are warned when one is coming.

Florida has played a big part in the space program. In 1958, the United States began launching spacecrafts from Cape Canaveral, in Florida. The first one was a small satellite. Bigger spacecrafts were sent up. Some carried people. In 1969 astronauts took a very long trip from Cape Canaveral. They went to the moon and back!

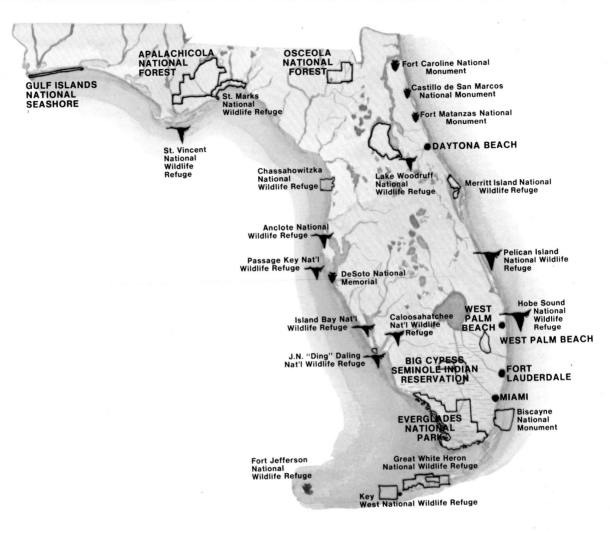

GULF ISLANDS NATIONAL SEASHORE

APALACHICOLA NATIONAL FOREST

OSCEOLA NATIONAL FOREST

Fort Caroline National Monument

Castillo de San Marcos National Monument

Fort Matanzas National Monument

St. Marks National Wildlife Refuge

St. Vincent National Wildlife Refuge

Chassahowitzka National Wildlife Refuge

DAYTONA BEACH

Lake Woodruff National Wildlife Refuge

Merritt Island National Wildlife Refuge

Anclote National Wildlife Refuge

Pelican Island National Wildlife Refuge

Passage Key Nat'l Wildlife Refuge

DeSoto National Memorial

Island Bay Nat'l Wildlife Refuge

Caloosahatchee Nat'l Wildlife Refuge

WEST PALM BEACH

Hobe Sound National Wildlife Refuge

WEST PALM BEACH

J.N. "Ding" Daling Nat'l Wildlife Refuge

BIG CYPRESS SEMINOLE INDIAN RESERVATION

FORT LAUDERDALE

MIAMI

Biscayne National Monument

EVERGLADES NATIONAL PARK

Fort Jefferson National Wildlife Refuge

Great White Heron National Wildlife Refuge

Key West National Wildlife Refuge

You have learned about some of Florida's history. Now it is time for a trip—in words and pictures—through the Sunshine State.

Pretend you are in an airplane high above Florida. Do you see that huge body of water stretching far to the east? That is the Atlantic Ocean. If you fly far enough, you'll see that the state is bounded by water on three sides.

Tampa, the third largest city in Florida

Your airplane is landing in a big city in northeast Florida. This is Jacksonville. Like many of Florida's big cities, Jacksonville lies on the Atlantic Ocean.

Once, Timucua Indians lived in this area. The French tried to settle here in 1564. They built Fort Caroline. You can visit this rebuilt fort in Jacksonville. The Spanish drove the French out in 1565. Americans built the town in the 1820s. It was named Jacksonville after Andrew Jackson, a U.S. president.

Today, Jacksonville is Florida's biggest city in number of people. It is also the biggest in size. Its 840 square miles make it one of the largest cities in the United States.

21

The St. Johns River runs through the city of Jacksonville.

Many insurance companies make their home in Jacksonville. Foods, paint, and paper are three products made in the city. Jacksonville is one of the main cities in the southeastern United States for shipping products. Some go by train from Jacksonville. Others go by boat.

Visit the Jacksonville Museum of Arts and Sciences. There you can see fossils and learn about the stars. At

22

Castillo de San Marcos

the Cummer Gallery of Art and the Jacksonville Art Museum you can see fine paintings. The University of North Florida and Jacksonville University are also in Jacksonville.

About 40 miles south of Jacksonville visit St. Augustine. St. Augustine is the oldest city in the United States. It was founded in 1565.

Visit the Castillo de San Marcos (kas • TEE • yo DAY SAN MARK • oss) in St. Augustine. This big fort really looks old. It should! The Spanish started building it in 1672. It is the oldest stone fort in the United States.

The Sanchez House in St. Augustine

It's exciting to walk through the narrow streets of St. Augustine. You'll see very old houses, churches, and schools. The Fountain of Youth Park will remind you of Ponce de León. The St. Augustine Lighthouse is also very pretty. It helps guide ships to shore.

From St. Augustine, go down the eastern coast of Florida along the Atlantic Ocean. Whether stormy or calm, the ocean is beautiful. In storms, many ships have sunk off the Florida coast. Some carried gold or silver.

Above: Cape Canaveral National
        Seashore and the Atlantic Ocean

Florida has many birds.
Left: A brown pelican in Everglades
        National Park
Right: Sandhill cranes in Myakka
        River State Park

Some people dive into the coastal waters in search of sunken treasure. A few find it.

Today, you'll see fishing boats off the coast. Shrimps, lobsters, oysters, and pompano are some of the seafoods caught in Florida waters.

Some birds fish, too! You'll see birds called pelicans. They dive into the water and catch fish in their big pouches. At Pelican Island, on the east coast of Florida, there are thousands of these birds. Herons and cranes also catch fish.

At Sea World, near Orlando, you can see some of the ocean animals. Left: A killer whale performs.

Many animals live *in* the ocean. Whales can be seen floating by the Florida coast. There are dolphins. Dolphins are very smart. They have been known to pull drowning people to shore. Sea cows, or manatees, live in the coastal bays and rivers. From a distance, some people have thought they were mermaids! These big, gentle animals have almost been wiped out. If you see one, you may notice a scar on its back. They are often hit—and killed—by motorboats.

You could spend a lifetime learning about the animals that live in or near the ocean.

The city of Daytona Beach is about 55 miles south of St. Augustine. Car races are held there, at the Daytona International Speedway. You also might see cars driven on the beaches. The beaches have hard-packed sand, and are almost as smooth as highways.

South of Daytona Beach visit Cape Canaveral. Many U.S. satellites and spaceships have been launched from there. In 1969, men were first sent to the moon from there. Would you like to see how spaceships are put together and launched? Would you like to see some spacecrafts? You can see all that at the John F. Kennedy Space Center at Cape Canaveral.

Right: Space vehicles at Kennedy Space Center
Below: Prickly pear cactus in Cape Canaveral National Seashore

Walt Disney World is near Orlando. Above is
Main Street and left is Cinderella's Castle
in Fantasy Land.

About 50 miles west of Cape Canaveral, visit the city
of Orlando. A huge amusement park is nearby. It is
called Walt Disney World, and it is as big as some towns.
Sea World is also in Orlando. You can see dolphins,
whales, sharks, and other sea animals there.

When traveling through the Orlando area of central
Florida, you'll see many orange groves. You can go for
miles and see nothing but orange trees. Florida is the
leading state for growing oranges.

Some Florida oranges are sent to factories. There they
are made into canned orange juice. Others are sent to
stores, where people buy them for eating.

When traveling through Florida, you can see many citrus trees.

You'll also see grapefruit trees in central Florida. Florida is the leading state for growing grapefruit. Lettuce, celery, tomatoes, and sugar cane are four other Florida crops. Beans, cucumbers, and watermelons are also grown in the state.

You might be surprised at the number of cattle ranches in central Florida. You'll see large herds of beef cattle. You'll also see cows that give milk. You could eat very well on food from Florida!

A shopping area in Palm Beach

From Orlando, head back to the Atlantic Coast. Continue south. You may notice that it's warmer in southern Florida than up in St. Augustine. It is often 75° in southern Florida in January. The fine weather of southeast Florida has made it a place of many growing cities. Vero Beach, West Palm Beach, Boca Raton, (BOH • kah reh • TAHN) and Fort Lauderdale are four towns you'll see in southeast Florida. All along the beaches you'll see big apartment buildings. You'll see many hotels.

People who come to vacation in an area are called *tourists.* Tourism is the number-one business in Florida.

Visit Miami, in southeast Florida. Each year, over 12 million tourists from all over the world visit the Miami area. At nearby Miami Beach you'll see "Hotel Row." It is a string of hotels along the ocean.

Miami also has many people who live there year round. It is Florida's second biggest city. Greater Miami— which counts its suburbs—has many more people than Jacksonville.

You'll notice that many people in Miami speak Spanish. Many people from Cuba, which is about 200 miles away, have moved to Miami.

A boat marina in Biscayne Bay with the skyline of Miami in the background

A famous and beautiful race track near Miami is called Hialeah Park.

There are many interesting places to visit in and near Miami. Visit the Miami Parrot Jungle. Parrots and other birds may land on your arm. Monkey Jungle is fun, too. There, *you* get into a cage and watch the monkeys run free! Miami is also a big sports area. Did you ever see the Orange Bowl football game on New Year's Day? It is played at the Orange Bowl in Miami. A pro football team, the Miami Dolphins, plays in the Orange Bowl, too.

Above: A Miccosukee Indian family
Left: A Miccosukee Indian woman sewing clothing

About 25 miles west of Miami visit the Miccosukee (mick • ah • SOO • key) Indian Reservation. There you can see woodcarving and other Indian crafts. The Seminoles also have reservations in Florida.

In all, there are about 7,000 Indians from about 35 different tribes in Florida today. Some Indians farm. Some raise cattle. Others work as teachers, police, and at many other jobs.

Much of the Indian culture is alive. Indian children learn the Indian language as well as English. At harvest time, some Indians hold the "Green Corn Dance." This is their time of Thanksgiving.

Key West is the farthest island from the Florida mainland.

Some Indians in Florida live in modern houses. Others still live in *chickees*. These houses are made with cypress poles which hold up palm-leaf roofs.

South of the Miccosukee Indian Reservation visit the Florida Keys. They are islands, strung like pearls below the mainland. You might wonder why these islands are called *keys*. The Spanish word *cayo* means *small island*. English-speaking people changed it to *key*.

You can travel from island to island on an overseas highway. Once, there were many fishermen and pirates in the Keys. The pirates are gone. But you'll still see fishermen.

John Pennekamp Coral Reef State Park

Key Largo is the first Florida Key you'll come to. It's
the largest of the Keys. Visit John Pennekamp Coral
Reef State Park near Key Largo. Most of this park is
underwater! Some people go there by diving underwater.
Others like to look at the corals through glass-bottomed
boats. Corals look like plants. But they are really made
of zillions of small animals that live close together.

Key West is the farthest southwest of the Keys.
Except for cities in Hawaii, Key West is farther south
than any other U.S. city. The author Ernest Hemingway
lived at Key West. You can visit the Ernest Hemingway
Home and Museum there.

Everglades National Park is the largest subtropical wilderness in the United States. Above is West Lake and to the right is the Pa-hay-okee Trail.

After seeing the Florida Keys, go back up to the mainland. Visit the Everglades, in the southern part of the mainland. The Everglades are a huge area of swamps and tall grass. People walk and canoe through the Everglades. The area is much like a jungle. You can see snakes, water birds, and 400-pound sea turtles. Bobcats prowl about the Everglades. You'll also see many alligators. They have sharp teeth and can grow over 12 feet long. You'll see alligators in many swampy places in southern Florida. People playing golf in Florida have been known to see alligators crawling along the course.

Above: Colorful flowers, such as
orchids, can be seen in Florida.
Left: An American alligator in
Nine-Mile Pond at Everglades
National Park

Just north of the Everglades is Big Cypress National
Preserve. You'll see many cypress trees there. They
grow where it is warm and wet. They live to be very
old—sometimes over 3,000 years. About half of Florida
is covered by forests. The state has many colorful trees,
such as pines and palms. Florida also has many kinds of
colorful flowers. Because of the warm weather, you can
see flowers in every season in Florida. Some of the
flowers grow nowhere else in the United States.

Canoeists in Myakka River State Park

After seeing the Everglades and Big Cypress National Preserve, head up the western coast of Florida. The body of water known as the Gulf of Mexico lies to the west. This part of Florida is often called the *Gulf Coast.*

There are many lovely islands off the Gulf Coast. Stop at Sanibel Island. You can go there by boat. Sanibel Island is known for the pretty seashells on its beaches.

Return to the mainland. North of Sanibel Island visit Gamble Mansion. It is a big plantation house, built in the 1840s. There are a number of plantations you can visit in Florida. Bulow Plantation Ruins and Kingsley Plantation are two of them.

Above: Florida Southern College in Lakeland
Left: The University of Tampa

North of Gamble Mansion you will come to the city of Tampa. The city lies on Tampa Bay.

Long ago, Timucua and Calusa Indians lived in the area. De Soto explored in the area in 1539. In 1824 the U.S. Army built Fort Brooke here. The city was formed around the fort.

Visit Busch Gardens in Tampa. It is a lovely zoo that has many pretty plants. If you like football, you can watch the Tampa Bay Buccaneers (buck • ah • NEARZ) play at Tampa Stadium. You'll see a lot of students in Tampa. The University of South Florida is there.

You'll see many fishing boats in Tampa Bay.
Fishermen bring back tons of shrimps. Cigars and
packaged foods are also made in the city.

Tampa has a "twin city" very near it. This is St.
Petersburg, also on Tampa Bay. Indian tools and
skeletons have been found here that are about 7,000
years old. The town began with a few farmers and cattle
ranchers in the 1840s. Today, St. Petersburg is one of
the largest cities in Florida. Boats and glass products are
made in the city. Lots of retired people live here.

In late winter and early spring, big league baseball teams practice. Teams train in St. Petersburg because of its fine weather. The city is nicknamed the *Winter Baseball Capital of the United States*. Teams also train in other Florida cities.

North of St. Petersburg stop at the town of Tarpon Springs. In the early 1900s, sponge fishermen from Greece came there. Greek sponge fishermen still live there. They dive deep into the ocean to gather sponges. A sponge is an animal that can hold a lot of water. People use them for cleaning.

State lawmakers
meet in the Capitol building
in Tallahassee.

Head up to the city of Tallahassee, in northwest
Florida. Tallahassee is the capital of Florida.

Visit the Capitol building. It is a 22-story skyscraper,
completed in 1977. Today, Florida lawmakers are
working to make better schools. They are working on the
problems of growing cities. They are working to protect
Florida's air, water, and wildlife.

Finish your Florida trip by visiting Wakulla (wah •
KOO • lah) Springs, a few miles outside Tallahassee. A
spring is water that bubbles out of the earth from a
crack in the ground.

Lovely sunsets are common along Florida's west coast.

The land of sunshine . . . alligators . . . and lovely
trees and flowers.

A state where you can see the John F. Kennedy Space
Center . . . Walt Disney World . . . and Sea World.

Home to Indians . . . retired people . . . farmers . . .
ranchers . . . and many others.

The leading orange-growing state.

This is Florida—the Sunshine State.

Facts About FLORIDA

Area—58,664 square miles (22nd biggest state)

Greatest Distance North to South—447 miles

Greatest Distance East to West—361 miles

Borders—Alabama and Georgia on the north; the Atlantic Ocean on the east;
the Straits of Florida on the south; the Gulf of Mexico and Alabama on the
west

Highest Point—345 feet above sea level (in Walton County, in northwest
Florida)

Lowest Point—Sea level, along the coast of the Atlantic Ocean

Hottest Recorded Temperature—109° (at Monticello, on June 29, 1931)

Coldest Recorded Temperature—Minus 2° (at the capital city of Tallahassee,
on February 13, 1899)

Statehood—Our 27th state, on March 3, 1845

Origin of Name Florida—Florida means *full of flowers* in Spanish; Ponce de
León gave the area this name

Capital—Tallahassee

Counties—67

U.S. Senators—2

U.S Representatives—19

State Senators—40

State Representatives—120

State Song—"Swanee River" by Stephen Foster

State Motto— *In God We Trust*

Main Nickname—The Sunshine State

Other Nicknames—The Orange State, the Peninsula State, the Everglade
State, the Flower State, the Alligator State

State Seal—Adopted in 1868

State Flag—Adopted in 1899

State Flower—Orange blossom

State Bird—Mockingbird

State Tree—Sabal palm

Some Rivers—St. Johns, Indian, Kissimmee, Suwannee, Escambia,
Apalachicola, Caloosahatchee, Peace, Aucilla, Blackwater, St. Marys,
Perdido

Lakes—Over 30,000

Biggest Lake—Lake Okeechobee (it is the second biggest freshwater lake
entirely in the United States)

Some Islands—Florida Keys, Sanibel, Ten Thousand, Santa Rosa, Merritt,
Hutchinson, St. George

National Forests—3

Animals—Black bears, deer, foxes, raccoons, opossums, otters, wildcats,
Florida panthers, rabbits, alligators, turtles, lizards, snakes, frogs, pelicans,
herons, egrets, many other kinds of birds

Fishing—Shrimps, lobsters, crabs, clams, oysters, scallops, red snappers,
    mackerel, catfish, pompano, mullet
Farm Products—Oranges, grapefruit, tangerines, limes, peanuts, pecans,
    soybeans, sugar cane, corn, tomatoes, tobacco, bananas, avocados,
    pineapples, strawberries, watermelons, cantaloupes, beef cattle, milk, hogs
Mining—Phosphate rock, oil, limestone, kaolin, zircon
Manufacturing Products—Frozen orange juice and many other packaged and
    frozen foods, chemicals, electronics equipment, missiles, paper products,
    wood products, glass products, metal products
Population—9,746,421 (1980 census)

Major Cities—		
Jacksonville	540,920	(1980 census)
Miami	346,865	
Tampa	271,523	
St. Petersburg	238,647	
Fort Lauderdale	153,279	
Hialeah	145,254	
Orlando	128,291	
Hollywood	121,323	

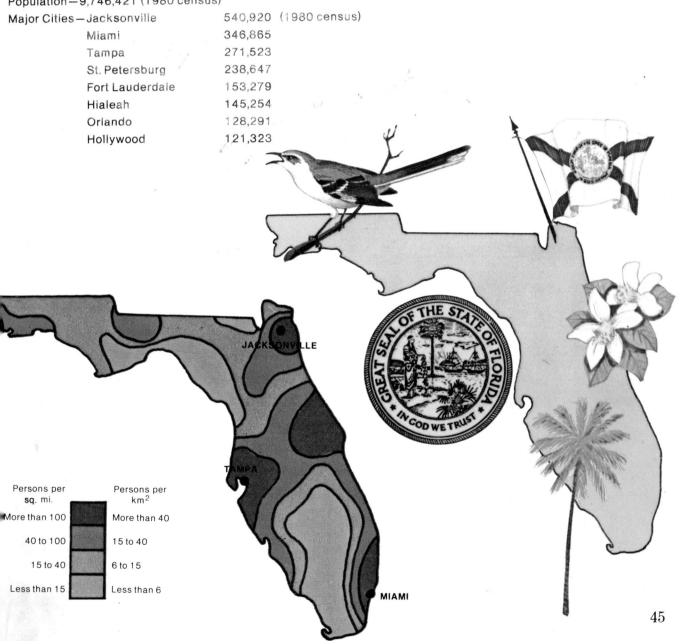

Persons per sq. mi.	Persons per km²
More than 100	More than 40
40 to 100	15 to 40
15 to 40	6 to 15
Less than 15	Less than 6

GREAT SEAL OF THE STATE OF FLORIDA
IN GOD WE TRUST

JACKSONVILLE
TAMPA
MIAMI

Florida History

There were people in Florida at least 10,000 years ago.

1513—Ponce de León arrives, names the land *Florida*, and claims it for Spain

1521—Ponce de León returns and tries to start a colony, but he is wounded in a fight with the Indians, and dies soon after

1528—Spaniard Pánfilo de Narváez explores Florida in search of gold

1539—Spaniard Hernando de Soto explores Florida

1564—French build Fort Caroline near where Jacksonville now stands

1565—Spanish found St. Augustine, now the oldest town in the United States; the Spanish then drive out the French

1586—Englishman Sir Francis Drake burns St. Augustine

1672—Spanish in St. Augustine begin work on the Castillo de San Marcos, which is now the oldest stone fort in the United States

1763—The English take control of Florida

1783—Spain regains control

1816-1818—In the First Seminole War, Indians are defeated by U.S. soldiers under General Andrew Jackson

1821—Florida passes to U.S. control

1822—Territory of Florida is created

1824—Tallahassee is chosen as Florida capital

1835-1842—During the Second Seminole War, Osceola and many of the Indians are killed; many leave Florida, but some remain

1845—On March 3, Florida becomes our 27th state

1850—Population of Florida is 87,445

1853—University of Florida is founded

1861—On January 10, Florida leaves the Union and soon joins the Confederacy; the Civil War begins on April 12

1864—Florida men help the Confederates win the Battle of Olustee, on February 20

1865—In March, Florida men help defend the capital city of Tallahassee; but by April the Confederates have lost the Civil War

1868—Florida again becomes part of the United States

1894-1895—Winter "Great Freeze" ruins citrus crops in northern Florida; many fruit growers move farther south

1900—Population of Florida reaches 528,542

1901—Jacksonville nearly destroyed by fire

1906-1907—Work begins to drain the Everglades in Fort Lauderdale area

1914-1918—During World War I, 42,030 Floridians serve for U.S.

1920-1925—People pour into Florida and build new towns

1928—About 1,800 die as a result of a hurricane and floods that hit Lake Okeechobee area

1935—In another hurricane, winds reach to about 200 miles per hour in the Florida Keys

1938—Overseas Highway to Key West opens

1939-1945—During World War II, over 250,000 Florida men and women
        serve; the state also supplies food and ships for the war effort
1947—Everglades National Park is established
1958—First U.S. space satellite, *Explorer I,* is launched from Cape Canaveral
        on January 31
1961—First U.S. spacecraft to carry a person is launched from Cape
        Canaveral
1969—First spacecraft to land people on the moon, *Apollo 11,* is launched
        from Cape Canaveral
1970—Population of the Sunshine State reaches 6,789,443
1976—Seminole Indians are paid 16 million dollars for lands taken during the
        1800s
1977—New 22-story state Capitol building is completed at Tallahassee
1980—Over 30 people die as a large boat knocks part of the Sunshine
        Skyway Bridge into Tampa Bay; racial riots occur in Miami; thousands
        of Cuban refugees arrive in Florida
1984—Citrus canker causes the destruction of millions of citrus trees

INDEX

agriculture, 16, 29
Alabama, 11
alligators, 36
animals, 26, 28, 32, 36
Apalachee Indians, 5
astronauts, 19, 27
Atlantic Ocean, 20, 21, 24
baseball, 41
Big Cypress National Preserve, 37
bird, state, 45
birds, 25, 32, 36
Boca Raton, 30
Bulow Plantation Ruins, 38
Busch Gardens, 39
Calusa Indians, 5, 39
Cape Canaveral, 19, 27
capital, state, 13, 42
Capitol building, 42
car races, 27
Castillo de San Marcos, 23
cattle, 29
chickees (Indian houses), 34
cities (map), 20
Civil War, 14, 15
Confederate States, 14
Coral Reef State Park, 35
corals, 35
cotton, 13, 16
crops, 16, 29, 40 (map)
Cuba, 7, 31
Cummer Gallery of Art, 23
cypress trees, 37
Daytona Beach, 27
Daytona International
    Speedway, 27

De Soto, Hernando, 39
Disney World, 28
dolphins, 26, 28
Drake, Sir Francis, 9
English, 10
Everglades, 36
explorers, 6, 39
farming, 16, 29
First Seminole War, 10, 11
fish and fishing, 25, 34, 40, 41
flag, state, 45
Florida, derivation of name, 6
Florida Keys, 34, 35
flower, state, 45
flowers, 37
football, 32, 39
forests, 17, 37
Fort Brooke, 39
Fort Caroline, 8, 21
Fort Lauderdale, 17, 30
Fountain of Youth, 6, 24
Fountain of Youth Park, 24
French 8, 21
fruits, 16, 17, 28, 29
Gamble Mansion, 38
Georgia, 11
gold, 6, 7
grapefruit, 16, 29
Greater Miami, 31
"Green Corn Dance," 33
Gulf Coast, 38
Gulf of Mexico, 38
Hemingway, Ernest, 35
Hemingway, Ernest, Home and
    Museum, 35
highways (map), 41

history of state, 3-20
"Hotel Row," 31
hurricanes, 18, 19
Indians, 5, 6, 9-13, 21, 33, 34,
    39
islands, 34, 35, 38
Jackson, Andrew, 21
Jacksonville, 21-23
Jacksonville Art Museum, 23
Jacksonville Museum of Arts
    and Sciences, 22
Jacksonville University, 23
Kennedy, John F., Space
    Center, 27
Key Largo, 35
keys, 34, 35
Key West, 35
Kingsley Plantation, 38
lakes (map), 20
Lighthouse, St. Augustine, 24
logging, 17
manatees (sea cows), 26
maps:
    cities, 20
    crops, 40
    highways, 41
    lakes, 20
    population, 45
    rivers, 20
    state symbols, 45
    transportation, 41
mastodons, 4
Menéndez de Aviles, Pedro, 8
mermaids, 26
Mexico, 7, 9
Miami, 17, 31, 32

INDEX, Cont'd

Miami Dolphins, 32
Miami Parrot Jungle, 32
Miccosukee Indian
  Reservation, 33
missions, 9
Monkey Jungle, 32
museums, 22, 23, 35
national preserve, 27
Natural Bridge, battle, 15
nickname, state, 3
Olustee, battle, 14, 15
Orange Bowl football game, 32
oranges, 16, 17, 28
Orlando, 28
Osceola, 12
Parrot Jungle, 32
Pelican Island, 25
pelicans, 25
Pennekamp, John, Coral Reef
  State Park, 35
pine trees, 17
pirates, 9, 34
plantations, 13, 38
Ponce de León, 6, 7, 24
population, 33, 45 (map)
presidents of the United States,
  21
Puerto Rico, 6

reservations, Indian, 33
rivers (map), 20
saber-toothed tigers, 4
St. Augustine, 8, 9, 23, 24, 30
St. Augustine Lighthouse, 24
St. Petersburg, 40, 41
Sanibel Island, 38
sea cows (manatees), 26
seafoods, 25
seal, state, 45
seashells, 38
Sea World, 28
Second Seminole War, 10, 12,
  13
Seminole Indians, 10-12, 33
Seminole Wars, 10-13
slavery, 13, 14, 15
"Slave State," 13
space program, 19, 27
Spanish, 6-10, 21, 23
Spanish-speaking people, 31
sponges, 41
sports, 32, 39, 41
statehood, 13
state park, 35
"States' Rights," 14
sugar, 13
"Sunshine State," 3

swamps, 36
Tallahassee, 13, 15, 42
Tampa, 17, 39, 40
Tampa Bay, 39, 40
Tampa Bay Buccaneers, 39
Tampa Stadium, 39
Tarpon Springs, 41
Tequesta Indians, 5
tigers, saber-toothed, 4
Timucua Indians, 5, 21, 39
tourists, 30, 31
transportation (map), 41
treasure, sunken, 24-25
tree, state, 45
trees, 17, 37
turpentine, 17
underwater park, 35
United States of America, 10
University of North Florida, 23
University of South Florida, 39
Vero Beach, 30
Wakulla Springs, 42
Walt Disney World, 28
weather, 18, 19, 30
West Palm Beach, 30
whales, 26, 28
"Winter Baseball Capital of the
  United States," 41
zoo, 39

About the Author:

Dennis Fradin attended Northwestern University on a creative writing scholarship and was graduated in 1967. While still at Northwestern, he published his first stories in *Ingenue* magazine and also won a prize in *Seventeen's* short story competition. A prolific writer, Dennis Fradin has been regularly publishing stories in such diverse places as *The Saturday Evening Post, Scholastic, National Humane Review, Midwest,* and *The Teaching Paper.* He has also scripted several educational films. Since 1970 he has taught second grade reading in a Chicago school—a rewarding job, which, the author says, "provides a captive audience on whom I test my children's stories." Married and the father of three children, Dennis Fradin spends his free time with his family or playing a myriad of sports and games with his childhood chums.

About the Artists:

Len Meents studied painting and drawing at Southern Illinois University and after graduation in 1969 he moved to Chicago. Mr. Meents works full time as a painter and illustrator. He and his wife and child currently make their home in LaGrange, Illinois.

Richard Wahl, graduate of the Art Center College of Design in Los Angeles, has illustrated a number of magazine articles and booklets. He is a skilled artist and photographer who advocates realistic interpretations of his subjects. He lives with his wife and two sons in Libertyville, Illinois.